Vaughan & Lucy Aandahl
1228 Jasmine St.
Denver, Colorado 80220

D0871219

STRINGS ON YOUR FINGERS

Gabriel Gély

STRINGS ON YOUR FINGERS

HOW TO MAKE STRING FIGURES

HARRY AND ELIZABETH HELFMAN

ILLUSTRATED BY
WILLIAM MEYERRIECKS

WILLIAM MORROW & COMPANY
NEW YORK 1965

for the children of
the Woodward School

Copyright © 1965 by Harry S. Helfman and Elizabeth C. Helfman

All rights reserved.

Published simultaneously in the Dominion of Canada
by George J. McLeod Limited, Toronto.

Printed in the United States of America.

Library of Congress Catalog Card Number 65-11329.

5   75   74   73   72

CONTENTS

ABOUT STRING FIGURES

Throw a spear of string from one hand to the other. Bounce a sleeping man out of a string bed. Make a parachute between your fingers. You can do all of these things with string figures.

A string figure is made with a loop of string about six and a half feet long, held taut between the hands. With the fingers of one hand you pick up loops of string from the other hand in different ways, over and over again. You may even use your teeth to pick up string. Fascinating designs are formed, change, and are formed again.

Making string figures is one of the oldest amusements in the world. For hundreds, and in some cases thousands, of years, people in many different parts of the world have worked out complicated sets of designs, using nothing more than a loop of string between their fingers.

Of course, the string that people used for these figures was often quite different from ours. In the far North string might have been made from animal sinews or strips of animal skin. In the tropical jungles it was often made from the long, tough vines that grew there.

The only string figure that is well known in this part of the world is the cat's cradle. Almost everyone knows how to make it or has watched other people do it. For some reason, this one figure has come down to us from long-ago times, probably by way of Asia. There are variations in the pattern of cat's cradle, but it is always done by two people. Each person picks up the loops of string in different ways with his fingers and transfers the string to his own hands, forming a new design each time.

Most string figures in other parts of the world are made by only one person. Primitive people everywhere invented string figures to represent familiar things around them. Probably these figures were made casually at first, one after another, until one appeared that reminded the maker of something. "Look, a spear!" Or, "That looks like the reeds down by the river!"

The names of these figures tell us something about the people who made them—the tools they used, the food they grew, what they thought about the world around them, and even the spirits they believed in. One figure is called Throwing a Spear; it was made by people who had considerable experience in doing just that. Another is the Yam Thief, which comes from a part of the world where the people farmed yams.

A surprising amount of action goes on in these figures. A fly disappears before it can be squashed between the hands. A thief makes a clean getaway. Two Eskimo boys run away from a house that has just collapsed. The maker of string figures sometimes invents stories as the designs change between his fingers. Soon he has an illustrated tale with which to entertain other people. These figures may have been the first moving pictures!

Sometimes string figures were made for magic. The Eskimos in the Hudson Bay region of North America made a magic string design in late autumn when the sun sank into the western arctic sky earlier each day. The design was a net of string between the hands, to catch the sun and keep it from going away so soon.

The Eskimos believed that magic could work in other ways, too. Boys were not allowed to play string games, because their fingers might get tangled in the strings. Then they would be sure to get them tangled in the harpoon line later on, when they were throwing the harpoon to catch seal, walrus, or whale.

Some Eskimos believed that it was dangerous for anyone to play these games too much. The "spirit of the strings" might get a person into its power. A crackling sound in the hut meant that this unseen spirit had arrived. Those inside

9

the hut were breathless with fear. Quickly they raised their hands with the string around them, and again and again, faster and faster, made the same figure the spirit was making with its invisible string. The trick was to beat the spirit at his own game; then he would go away.

On the other side of the world, on the island of New Guinea, people planted yams for countless years and watched hopefully for the green shoots to come up out of the earth. Tall sticks were put in the ground for the yam vines to wind around. Everyone, children too, made string figures while they watched the yams. Making the right figures, they believed, might help the yam shoots to climb neatly around the sticks.

Not far from New Guinea, in the Fiji Islands of the southwest Pacific Ocean, other string figures were popular. The Fiji women made the figure of Lulu, the owl, in string. While they made it they chanted:

> "The owl soars on high;
> The rat shakes in fear of death
> In the long grass."

They thought these words might help the owl catch the rat.

The Maoris of New Zealand created very complicated string figures. Some of them were made by three or four people, using an enormous loop of cord. Maori figures often illustrated great deeds done by heroes of mythology.

Farther east in the Pacific Ocean, on Easter Island, tales are still told and illustrated by a complicated series of string figures. In this way the folklore of the people is brought to life for everyone to learn and enjoy.

In West Africa, the Ashanti had a traditional string figure called the Reeds Along the River Tano. While their fingers were busy with the strings, the people sang a song about the river, "Pure, pure Tano."

However, if you ask a West African of today what he knows about string games, he may only remember that he used to play them when he was a child. The chances are that his fingers can still make the patterns of the string games he used to play, but he probably has forgotten their meaning.

Some of the African string figures are the same as those done on islands in the Pacific Ocean or by the Eskimos in the far North. This does not mean that people in different parts of the world traveled great distances and taught their string games to other people. Amazing as it seems, the same figures developed by themselves in widely separated places. The names and meanings of the figures varied. For example, the figure called a Fish Spear by the people of

11

New Guinea was also made by Indians on the northwest coast of North America, but they called it Pitching a Tent.

The American Indians invented a great variety of string figures. One made by Indians in Oregon showed two boys fighting for an arrow. Another made by the Navajos imitated a zigzag figure of lightning. Shapes of stars appeared between their nimble fingers. One of their favorite figures represented a hogan, the home where the family shared their life, including the legends of their people.

Anthropologists, who study the everyday customs of people in many parts of the world, have found string figures interesting enough to collect in books. Hundreds of different figures have been described. Some of them are very complicated.

Even the anthropologists cannot always find out what string figures mean to the people who make them. But the meaning does not always matter. String figures can be made just for fun.

They can be useful, too. During World War II the U.S. Army advised soldiers and airmen in the South Pacific area to carry a loop of string with them. If a soldier was downed in a Pacific jungle, and an unfriendly native approached, he could get out his string and start playing cat's cradle.

The native, in turn, might borrow the string and show the soldier his own string figures. The chances are that the soldier and the native could not understand a single word of each other's language. But playing string games together was almost as good as talking.

This advice from the U.S. Army was not a wild idea. It had been tried before. Anthropologists have gone into territory where primitive people live, equipped with a loop of string. They have found that the sharing of string figures is a wonderful way of getting acquainted without words.

Try some of the string figures in this book, following the directions closely. Then try making up figures of your own. Start with one of the basic positions and go on from there, in your own way. What do your designs suggest to you? Not a fish spear or a yam vine! Perhaps a radio tower, a television aerial, or even a spaceship on its way to the moon.

GENERAL INSTRUCTIONS
Read This First!

To make string figures, all you need is a piece of heavy string about six and a half feet long. Tie it together at the ends with a square knot. To make a square knot, hold one end of the string in each hand. Put the end of the string in your right hand over the other end, then under it. Then put the end in your left hand over the right end, then under. The knot should look like this, with the ends turned back opposite each other and lying flat. After you have made the knot and pulled it tight, cut off the loose ends. Now you are ready to make string figures.

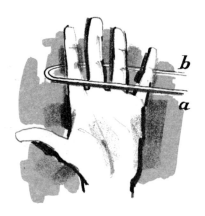

In the instructions certain terms appear frequently. The following diagrams will make them clear.

The near string (a) of a loop is the string nearer you. The far string (b) is the one farther from you. The near

14

side of any set of strings is the side nearer you. The far side is the side farther away.

The back of your finger or thumb is the side with the fingernail.

Many of the string figures described in this book start in the same way. We call this Position A. Some of the instructions tell you to take Position A, without describing it again. It is a good idea, therefore, to learn it before you begin doing the figures.

1. Place the loop of string on your hands as shown in the above drawing.

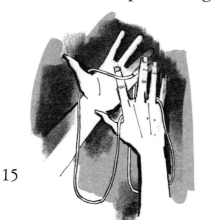

2. Put your right forefinger up under the left palm string. Spread out your hands, with the loop from the left palm string now on your right forefinger.

15

3. Take up the right palm string with your left forefinger in the same way. Draw your hands apart.

This is Position A.

Follow the instructions carefully, step by step. The easiest figures come first in the book, and they get harder as you go along. If you drop the wrong string, or pick up the wrong one, in

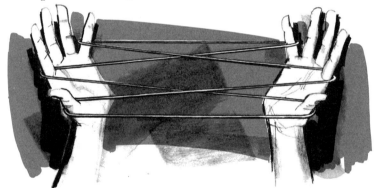

making any figure, start over again. It is almost impossible to correct a mistake, and it is a waste of time to try.

Except where the directions indicate otherwise, keep your hands upright at all times.

With a little practice you can become an expert.

16

THROWING A SPEAR

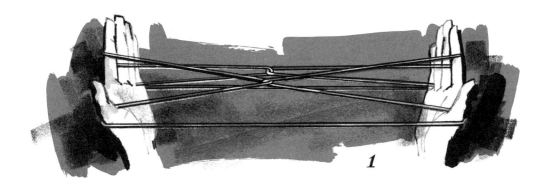

1

Try throwing a spear from one hand to another. You can do it again and again—with string. This figure comes from Australia and the islands of the Torres Strait, between New Guinea and northern Australia.

1. Take Position A. (Be sure to take your left palm string with your right forefinger first.)

2. Transfer the loop on your right forefinger to the tip of your left forefinger. Then move the original left forefinger loop over it onto your right forefinger. Draw your hands apart. (Diagram 1.)

3. Release the loop on your left forefinger. Draw your hands apart. Close your left fingers onto your palm. You now have a spear with a handle on the left and three prongs on the right. (Diagram 2.)

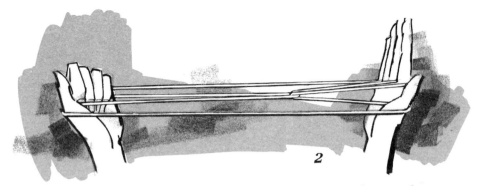

2

4. To throw the spear prongs to your left hand, open your left fist. Pass your left forefinger under the loop on your right forefinger without crossing any long strings. Draw your hands apart. Release the right forefinger loop. Draw your hands apart.

Thus you can throw the spear back and forth.

A THUMB CATCH

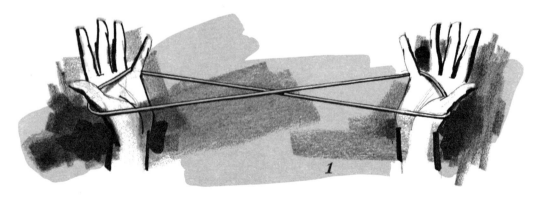

1

he Osage Indians of Oklahoma used to play a string game called Thumb Catch. You can make a thumb catch, too.

1. Put the string around the thumb and little finger of each hand, crossing the strings in an X between your hands. (Diagram 1.)

2. Take up the left palm string from underneath with your right forefinger. Draw your hands apart. Then take up the right palm string from underneath with your left forefinger. Draw your hands apart.

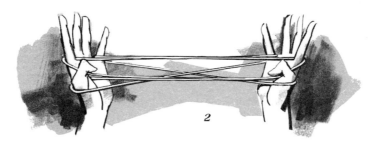

3. Bend your thumbs down over the near forefinger strings. (Diagram 2.)

4. Point your hands down. Hold the thumb strings tight against your palms. Drop the strings from your little fingers and from your forefingers. Turn your hands up and draw them apart. (Diagram 3.)

Each thumb now has a catch.

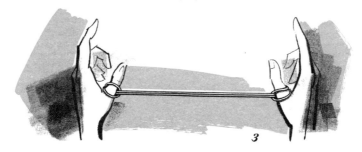

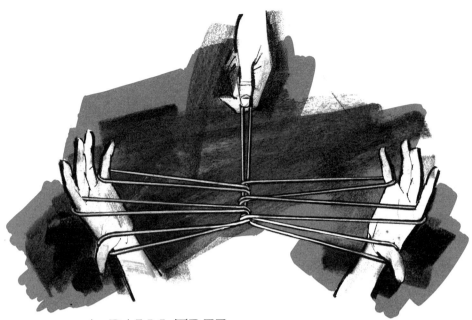

A PALM TREE

 This figure was also invented by people who live on islands in the Torres Strait.

1. Take Position A.

2. Pick up the far little finger string with your teeth. Draw it up toward you over the other strings, and hold it there.

3. Exchange the loops on your little fingers, passing the left loop over the right loop.

4. Exchange the loops on your forefingers the same way, passing the left loop over the right loop.

5. Exchange the loops on your thumbs the same way, passing the left loop over the right loop.

6. Slide the cross strings together as shown in the drawing. There is the palm tree.

If someone is on hand to help you, you can make the palm tree with him. After taking Position A, ask your friend to pick up your near thumb string and draw it away from you over all the other strings. He should hold it there while you continue with steps three through five. Then have him slide the cross strings together to form the palm tree.

THE EIFFEL TOWER

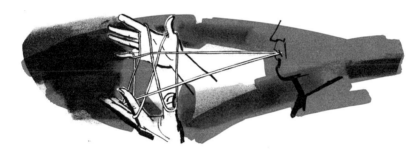

 his is a variation of the Palm Tree figure, with a modern interpretation.

1. Take Position A.

2. Pick up the far little finger string with your teeth.

3. Move your hands down and away from you. Then draw your hands apart with palms facing each other.

There is the Eiffel Tower. Or, if you like, it can be a radio tower.

21

A SIBERIAN HOUSE AND
TWO ESKIMOS RUNNING AWAY

 The Siberian House comes from the Eskimos, who are experts at making string figures. It is not as hard to do as it looks.

1. Take Position A.

2. Insert four fingers of each hand through the thumb loop on the same hand and press them against your palm.

3. Throw the near thumb string over both your clenched hands so that the string is behind your little fingers. Draw your hands apart so they face each other.

4. Move your thumbs away from you, over the near string which comes around from the back of each hand and under all the other strings.

5. On the back of your thumbs pick up the bottom little finger string. Return thumbs to original position, moving under all the strings except the bottom near strings.

6. With the thumb and forefinger of your right hand, pick up the string on the back of your left hand and drop it onto your palm. Do not drop it over your thumb and do not drop any other strings!

7. With your left hand, pick up the string on the back of your right hand and drop it onto your palm.

8. Point your fingers away from you. At the same time draw your hands apart. (Diagram 1.)

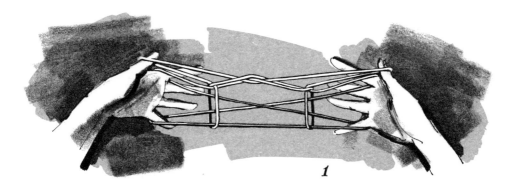

1

This figure is the Siberian House. It is not a strong house. In the next step it breaks into pieces. Two boys in the house escape by running away from the house and away from each other.

9. To show the house breaking and the boys running away, release the strings on your forefingers. Spread your hands slowly. Away they go! (Diagram 2.)

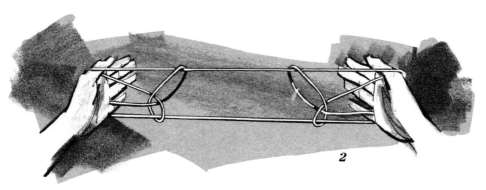

2

A FLY

In South America flies are pests, just as they are everywhere else in the world. South American Indians invented this string figure to show what they would like to do with the flies.

1. Loop the string around each thumb. Spread out your hands, holding them upright.

2. Move the fingers of your left hand down, counterclockwise, reaching under both strings. Pick up the strings on the back of your hand. You now have two strings across the back of your left hand, and none across the palm.

3. With the little finger of your right hand, pick up from the palm side both strings between the thumb and

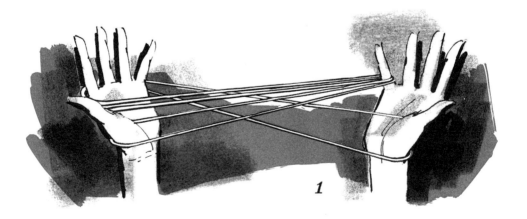

1

forefinger of your left hand. Then spread out your hands. Be careful not to drop the string from your left thumb! (Diagram 1.)

4. Move the little finger of your left hand over the top strings. Pick up, from the far side and underneath, both strings leading from your right thumb. Spread out your hands.

5. With your right thumb and forefinger, pick up the strings on the back of your left hand and drop them over your left fingers to the palm of your left hand. Do not drop any other strings on your fingers. Draw your hands apart. (Diagram 2.) The fly, with its body and wings, appears between your hands.

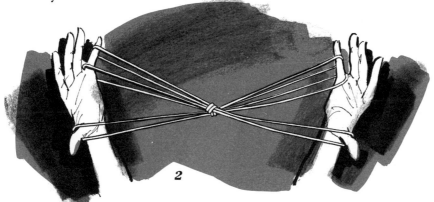

6. Clap your hands together to catch the fly. Release the strings on your little fingers. Draw your hands apart. The fly has gone!

A NOOSE

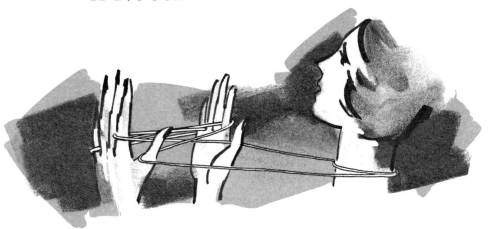

Here is a good trick to try on your friends. You can pretend to choke yourself with your loop of string. This trick comes from the Philippines and other islands in the Pacific Ocean.

1. Place the loop of string over your head so that it is hanging loose from your neck.

2. Pass the right string in front of you and to the left. Then put it over your head. You now have one string around your neck, and another loop hanging from it.

3. With the hanging string, form Position A. (Be sure to take the left palm string with your right forefinger first.)

4. Drop the little finger strings, holding your hands upright.

5. Put the loop formed by the forefinger strings over your head, so that the crossed strings are at the back of your head. Let the strings drop.

6. Gently pull on the hanging strings, as if you are trying to choke yourself. You will not choke. The loop will come away from your neck.

A HOGAN

A hogan is a Navajo Indian house. Here is how the Indians made a hogan of string.

1. Place a loop of string over the back of the forefinger and middle finger of your left hand. Leave a long loop hanging down on the palm side of your left hand. Keep your left hand upright.

2. Put your right hand under the near string and through the loop. With your right forefinger, pick up the string between the forefinger and middle finger of your left hand. Pull this string down all the way. Release your right forefinger. (Diagram 1.)

1

3. Put your right hand under the near string and through the loop, as before. With the thumb and forefinger of your right hand, take hold of the two strings between your left forefinger and middle finger. Pull these strings through the hanging loop and down all the way. Let the strings drop from your right hand.

4. Arrange the four strings on your left palm so that the knotted strings are on the outside. (Diagram 2.)

5. Pick up the string nearest your thumb and loop it behind your thumb. Pick up the string nearest your little finger and loop it behind your little finger. (Diagram 3.)

6. Move your left palm so it faces upward. With the

thumb and forefinger of your right hand, pick up the loop over the knots. Draw this string up as you lower your left hand. Be careful not to drop any strings from your left hand! (Diagram 4.)

This figure is a hogan. Or, if you like, it is a tent. Turn the hogan over, and you have a parachute. Let go of the long loops, and dangle the figure by the short loop. Now it is "a policeman's keys."

A MOTH

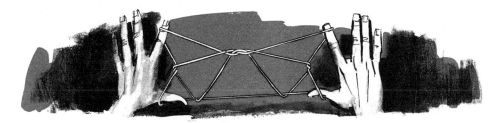

 The Zulus of South Africa had many string figures. Here is one, in the shape of a moth.

1. Take Position A.

2. Drop the thumb strings. Draw your hands apart.

3. Move your thumbs away from you over two strings. Pick up the near little finger strings on the back of your thumbs. Return your thumbs to the original position.

4. Drop the strings from your little fingers. Draw your hands apart.

29

5. Move your thumbs away from you. Pick up the near forefinger strings on the back of your thumbs. Return to the original position.

6. With the thumb and forefinger of your right hand, pick up the bottom string on the thumb of your left hand. Drop this string over your left thumb.

7. Do the same with the bottom string on your right thumb.

8. Put the tip of your forefingers into the close-together loops between your forefingers and thumbs. Press your fingers against your palms.

9. Move your hands down, dropping the loops from the back of your forefingers. Do not drop any other loops. Turn your hands down and stretch them wide.

This figure is the Zulu moth.

TWO DIAMONDS

 The Maoris of New Zealand loved to make diamonds in string, sometimes as many as six. Here is how they made two.

1. Take Position A.

2. Drop the thumb strings.

3. Cross over three strings with your thumbs. Pick up

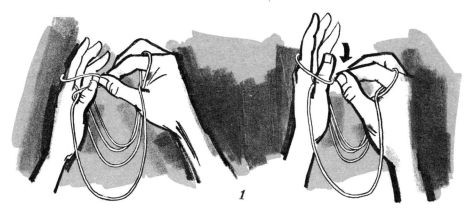

the far little finger strings with the back of your thumbs, and return.

4. With your right hand, pick up the left near forefinger string and loop it over your left thumb. (Diagram 1.)

5. Do the same thing with the string around your right forefinger.

6. Turn your thumbs down and slip the near thumb string to the far side of your thumb. (Diagram 2.)

7. Slacken the strings between your hands. Put the tip of your forefingers into the triangles near your thumbs. Press your forefingers against your palms.

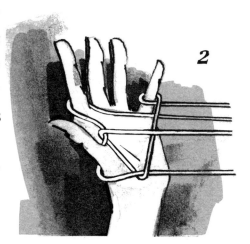

8. Drop the little finger strings.

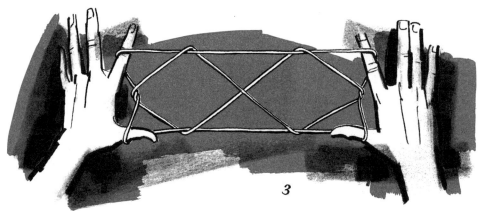

3

9. Pull the strings on your forefingers and thumbs taut. Turn your hands away from you and stretch them wide. (Diagram 3.)

There are the two diamonds.

A YAM THIEF

1

Here is a string trick that is known in many parts of the world. A story is always told with it. On the islands of the Torres Strait the story is about a thief who comes to steal the yams in a farmer's garden.

1. Hold your left hand in

a vertical position, and place the loop of string over your hand. (Diagram 1.) The knot should be at the bottom.

2. From the near side, put your right forefinger in back of the palm string.

3. Place this forefinger be- 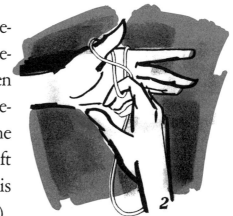 tween the thumb and fore- finger of your left hand. Then hook the tip of your right fore- finger over the top of the string on the back of your left hand. Pull a small loop of this string forward. (Diagram 2.)

4. With the thumb and forefinger of your right hand, twist this loop clockwise and place it over the forefinger of your left hand.

5. Pull both hanging strings, to tighten the loops on your left thumb and forefinger.

The loop on your thumb represents the owner of the yam patch. He is fast asleep after a hard day's work. The thief creeps up and starts tying the yams in bags, one after another. To represent the bags, loop the string over each finger in the following way.

6. From the near side, put your right forefinger in back of the palm string and then between your left forefinger

33

and middle finger. Again, hook the tip of your right fore-finger over the top of the string on the back of your left hand. Pull a small loop of this string forward (between forefinger and middle finger).

7. With the thumb and forefinger of your right hand, twist this loop clockwise and place it over the middle finger of your left hand. Tighten hanging strings.

3

8. Repeat these instructions until you also have a loop over the ring finger and little finger of your left hand. (Diagram 3.)

The owner of the yams wakes up. Something seems to be happening in the garden. He goes to look.

9. Take the loop off your left thumb. (This is the farmer waking up.) Hold this loop against your hand with your thumb.

The farmer sees the yams all tied up in tight bundles.

10. To show that the loops are tight, pull on the far hanging string. Let go of the loop you are holding with your thumb.

The thief comes sneaking back and sees the farmer.

11. Pull the near hanging string, quickly! (Diagram 4.) All the loops disappear. The thief has made off with the bags of yams.

This trick has been done by the Pygmies in Africa, several tribes of American Indians, the Alaskan Eskimos, and many other people. Sometimes the loops are said to represent a row of birds that fly away when something frightens them. To the Eskimos, the trick is a game of cat and mouse. You can make up your own story to fit the disappearing loops.

35

MAN ON A BED

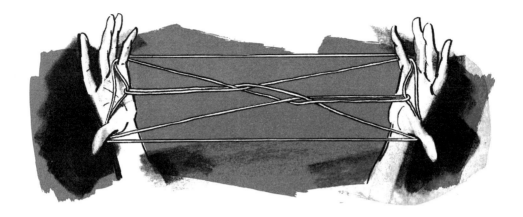

 Here is another figure from the people of the Torres Strait. In this one, a sleeping man is bounced right out of bed.

1. Take Position A. Keep the forefinger loops near the tip of your forefingers.

2. Move your thumbs away from you, under the forefinger loops. Pick up on the back of your thumbs the near little finger strings. Bring your thumbs back to the original position, passing under the forefinger loops.

3. Pass your little fingers through the forefinger loops from above. Pick up on the back of your little fingers the far thumb strings. Return your little fingers to the original position, taking back only the string just picked up.

4. Release the loops from your forefingers. Sing:

> Man on a bed,
> Man on a bed,
> Lies asleep,
> Lies asleep—
> Bed breaks!

At the word *breaks,* release the loops from your little fingers. Spread your hands wide. The man and the bed are gone!

THREADING A CLOSED LOOP

hreading this closed loop is a good trick, if you can do it. The Kwakiutl Indians of south-western Canada used it as a password. When they met in the forest, members of a certain secret society identified themselves by doing this trick.

Instead of the usual loop, this trick requires a piece of string eighteen inches long.

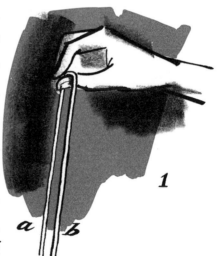

1. Hold the string in the middle, between the thumb and forefinger of your right hand. (Diagram 1.)

2. Grasp string (a) at its middle point with your left hand and make a fist around it.

3. With your right hand, wind the string above your left thumb toward you, wrapping it around your thumb three times.

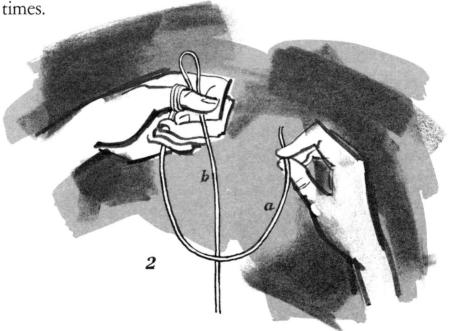

4. With your right hand, make a loop with string (b) and place this loop between the thumb and forefinger of your left hand. Hold it there and remove your right hand. Your left hand should be pointing to the right.

5. Pick up string (a) in front of string (b). (Diagram 2.)

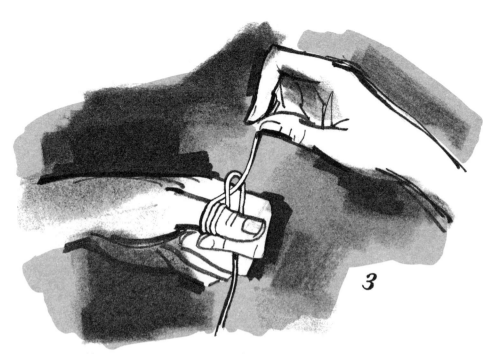

6. Pull up string (a) quickly, not through the loop, but between the thumb and forefinger of your left hand. Pull it up as far as it will go. Do not drop any strings. Keep holding the loop. (Diagram 3.)

The loop will appear to have been threaded by the right hand string.

CAT'S CRADLE

he cat's cradle is the best known string figure in Europe and most of North America. It is well known in Asia, too, and that is probably where it

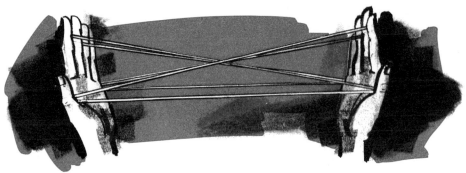

started. The Chinese call it "well rope"; the Koreans, "woof-taking"; the Japanese, "woof pattern string-taking." No one knows where the name "cat's cradle" came from.

The so-called cradle is really only the first step of cat's cradle. There are four well-known figures: cat's cradle, soldier's bed, cat's eye, and fish in a dish. The cradle is made by one person, and the other figures are made as two people alternately take the pattern off each other's hands in different ways.

Here are instructions for making the cat's cradle, which is the name of this step almost everywhere. The other figures follow it.

1. Put the string across the back of the four fingers of your right hand.

2. Do the same with your left hand. Spread out your hands.

3. With the back of your left hand, pick up the near string on your right hand by going over and then under it.

Draw your hands apart. You now have a palm string and two back strings on your left hand.

4. With your right hand, pick up the near string on your left hand and arrange it as you did the string on your left hand.

5. With the middle finger of your right hand, pick up, from underneath, the palm string of your left hand.

6. With the middle finger of your left hand, pick up, from underneath, the palm string of your right hand. Draw your hands apart.

This figure is the cat's cradle.

SOLDIER'S BED

The soldier's bed is sometimes called "the fish pond" in this country. In Korea it is "a chessboard"; in Japan it represents a domestic cat transforming itself into a mountain cat. In France it is "scissors"; and in England it is "a church window."

This figure is a continuation of the cat's cradle. It is done by a second person. He faces the first, who holds the cat's cradle upright on his fingers. The following instructions are from the point of view of the second person (B in Diagram 1). *Left* and *right* refer to his left and right, not that

41

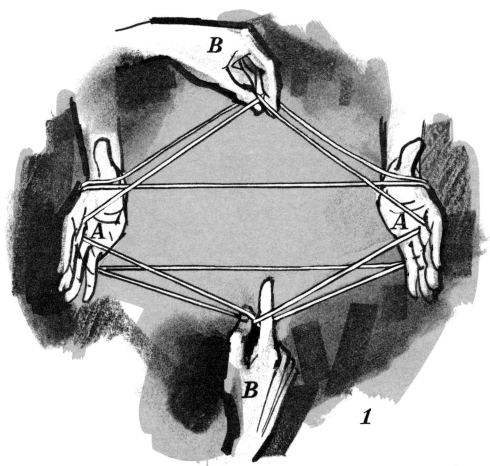

1

of the first person (A in Diagram 1). *Near* means near the second person, and *far* means far from him.

1. Approach the string figure from above. Put your left thumb under the right near middle finger string. Put your left forefinger under the left near middle finger string.

2. Bring your left thumb and forefinger together and pinch loosely between their tips the two near middle finger

42

strings where they cross. Keep holding these strings.

3. Keeping your hand above the string figure, put your right thumb behind the right far middle finger string. Put your right forefinger behind the left far middle finger string.

4. Bring your right thumb and forefinger together and pinch loosely between their tips the two far middle finger strings where they cross. (Diagram 1.)

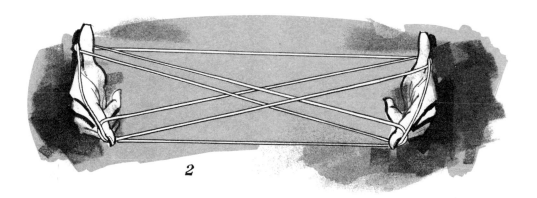

2

5. Holding these strings, bring your hands around the outside of the other strings, down, and up through the middle. Take the strings off your partner's hands. Spread out your hands, with your thumbs and forefingers as far apart as possible. (Diagram 2.)

There is the soldier's bed. Or it may be a mountain cat, or whatever it reminds you of.

43

CAT'S EYE

In England the cat's eye is called "diamonds." You will see why. In Korea it is "cow's eyeball" and, in Japan, "horse eye."

This figure is similar to the soldier's bed. It is done by the first person. He faces the second, who holds the soldier's bed upright on his fingers. The instructions are from the point of view of the first person.

1. This time the crossed strings are approached from underneath. Put your left thumb between the right near forefinger string and the right near thumb string. Put your left forefinger between the left near forefinger string and

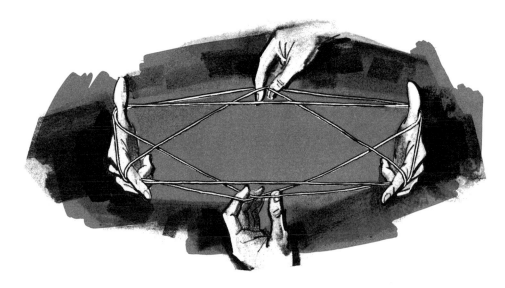

the left near thumb string. Pinch the strings where they cross.

2. Move your right hand over the strings to the far side of the string figure. From underneath, put your right thumb between the right far forefinger string and the right far thumb string. Put your right forefinger between the left far forefinger string and the left far thumb string. Pinch the strings on your partner's hand where they cross.

3. Holding these strings, bring your hands around the outside of the other strings, up, and down through the middle. Take the strings off your partner's hands. Spread out your hands, with your thumbs and forefingers as far apart as possible and pointing down.

This is the cat's eye.

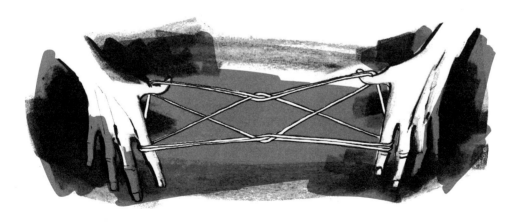

FISH IN A DISH

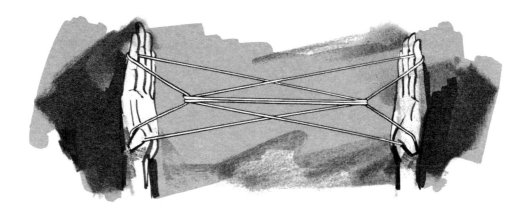

 This figure is done by the second person. He faces the first, who holds the cat's eye figure on his fingers.

1. Put your right thumb from above into the right far triangle of the cat's eye figure. Put your right forefinger from above into the left far triangle.

2. In the same way, put your left thumb into the right near triangle and your left forefinger into the left near triangle.

3. Pinch your thumbs and forefingers together. Turn them up through the center diamond. Spread out your hands and take the figure off the hands of the first person.

There is the fish in a dish.

If you have made all the string figures in this book, you are an expert. Now you can invent variations of your own. Or you might try making up a story, using some of these figures as illustrations. Here is an example.

One day a pilot named Sam discovered that his plane was out of gas. So he came down in a parachute. (Make the upside-down hogan figure for a parachute.) Sam landed on a tropical island, on top of a palm tree. (Make the palm tree.) He climbed down and explored. (The palm tree sways as he climbs down.)

Sam liked the island so much he decided to live there, so he made a tent. (The hogan figure makes a good tent.) All day long he swatted the flies and caught fish with a spear. (Make the disappearing-fly and the spear-throwing figures.) What did he do after that? Your story can go on and on.

BIBLIOGRAPHY

You can read more about string figures
in the following books.

Ball, W. W. Rouse, "String Figures" in *String Figures and Other Monographs.* New York, Chelsea Publishing Company, 1960.

Haddon, Kathleen, *Artists in String.* New York, Dutton, 1930.

Jayne, Caroline Furness, *String Figures and How to Make Them.* New York, Dover Publications, 1962, and Gloucester, Massachusetts, Peter Smith, 1963.